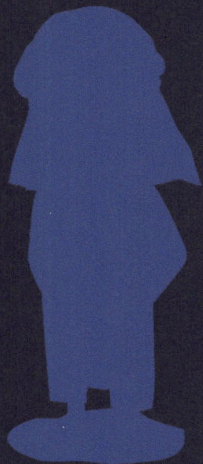

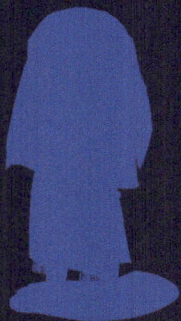

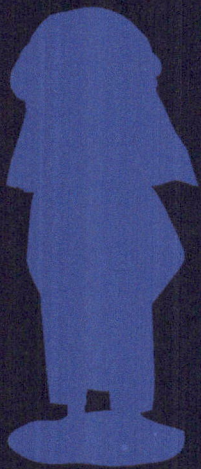

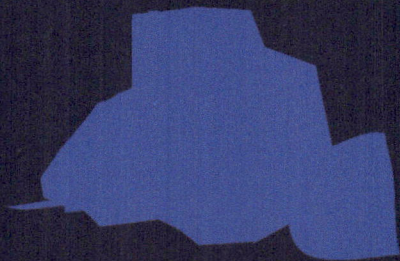

JOSEPH

Journey of A Dreamer

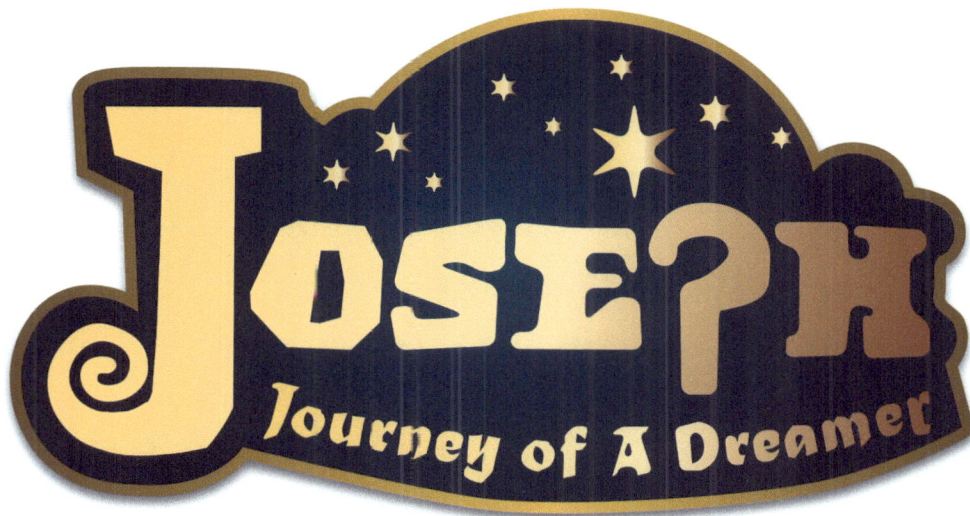

Brought to you by J GOSPEL

Dedicated to

LORD JESUS CHRIST

Foreword

Children of this generation are bombarded by distractions. Electronic and interactive devices have captivated their minds. Traditional Bible study groups may no longer retain the full interest of our youth.

I resigned as Pastor from a church and started J Gospel Net Inc. in 2006 to bring forth the Gospel and advance God's kingdom through Internet ministry. Especially for children born in this era, we want to bring them a fun way of learning words of God.

This graphic book (which also comes in e-book and app version) is designed for children between ages 6-12. It is a perfect material for children's Sunday school. By using this book, teachers can discuss with the children religious and everyday topics. It can also serve as a children's bedtime story that builds a bridge between parents and their children. Parents can provide guidance to children as they grow up through a story they both share.

We thank Lord for providing us with a team of talented and dedicated workers. May the Lord bless you and keep you.

Sincerely,
Rev. Roycos Hom
Founder of J Gospel Net Inc.

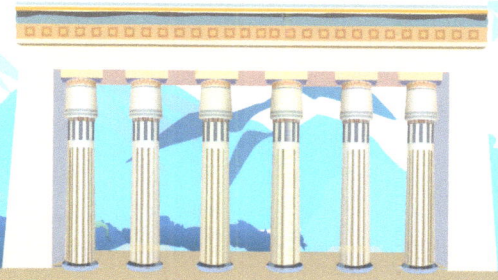

A long time ago, in the land of Canaan, lived a man called Jacob and his twelve sons. The mother of his two youngest sons, Joseph and Benjamin, had sadly passed away. Jacob had loved her very much, and for this reason, he had a soft spot for the two boys, especially Joseph.

Joseph was sweet and kind, and would often try to get his brothers to behave. But his brothers didn't like that. One day, Jacob gave Joseph a very special present: a colorful robe.

"Oh, I love it!" said Joseph, "Thank you, dad!" The older brothers started to grumble, "It's not fair!" they said, feeling jealous.

One morning, Joseph woke up feeling rather puzzled. "I had some very strange dreams," he said to his brothers, "we were gathering grain when suddenly, my bundle stood up. Then, your sheaves gathered around mine and bowed down to it!"

"My second dream is even more strange, I saw the sun surrounded by the moon and eleven stars, and all of a sudden, they all started to bow down to the sun! I wonder what it means."

The brothers looked at one another incredulous, "You want to reign over us!" they cried. And from that moment on, they started hating him even more.

Joseph's brothers would often take the family's flock to graze on lands far away. "Could you go and check on them?" Jacob asked Joseph one day. "Absolutely," he replied, and he started his journey. Joseph had no idea what was waiting for him on the other side.

"He's coming, let's kill him!" whispered one of the brothers. "No, no, no!" replied Reuben, who was the eldest, "Let's just give him a good scare. We'll throw him in this pit." I'll come and rescue him later, he thought. As soon as Joseph was close enough, the brothers grabbed him, tore his coat and threw him into the pit. But sadly, Reuben didn't have time to rescue him, as his brothers had sold him as a slave to two merchants passing by.

They then stained Joseph's coat with blood from a goat and they showed it to their father, "Joseph was killed by wild animals," they lied.

Joseph and the merchants traveled for days until they reached the land of Egypt. There, Joseph was sold to Potiphar, a powerful captain who worked for the king.

Joseph was now a slave for a man he didn't know, in a land that was not his own. He could have easily despaired, but instead, he prayed and asked God for help.

And God did indeed help him! As everything Joseph did, succeeded. Potiphar, his boss, noticed this and gave him more and more responsibilities.

Joseph, being a handsome man, was soon noticed by Potiphar's wife, who begged him to kiss her.

"I can't do that to my master!" said Joseph. He knew that what the woman was asking was against God's will. This angered Potiphar's wife, who soon came up with a plan to get her revenge.

During yet another attempt to steal a kiss, she grabbed Joseph's coat. She then showed it to her husband shouting, "Your servant tried to kiss me! He should go to prison!" Potiphar believed her, and Joseph was sent to jail.

Stuck in a cold, dark cell, Joseph, once again, prayed to the Lord asking for His help. God listened to his cry. Soon Joseph found favor in the eyes of the head jailer, who gave him important responsibilities.

One day, both Pharaoh's cupbearer and the baker had been caught doing something wrong and were sent straight to jail.

Life in prison was slow and monotonous, until one morning, when the cupbearer and the baker woke up feeling very upset. They both had had a very strange dream.

Joseph could see that they were upset, so he asked them to explain their dreams to him.

"I dreamt of a vine with three branches," said the cupbearer, "I made wine out of its grapes and I served it to the pharaoh."

"I, instead, dreamt of tree baskets full of baked goods that were balancing on my head," said the baker, "but a whole load of birds came and ate every single crumb."

After asking for God's help, Joseph gave the men the meaning of their dreams. "Your dream means that in three days you will be free," he said to the cupbearer, "and you'll go back working for Pharaoh."

"But you," he said, looking at the baker, "your dream means that in three days the king will get you killed."

Three days later, things happened exactly the way Joseph had predicted.

As the cupbearer was leaving the prison Joseph pleaded, "Please, tell Pharaoh about me!" But the cupbearer, in all his excitement, forgot all about Joseph.

Two years later, Pharaoh woke up feeling troubled by a strange dream he had. So he gathered all his wise men and explained, "I dreamt that I was near the river Nile when I saw seven fat cows coming out from the water. Suddenly seven thin cows came out, and they ate the fat ones." He then added, "I also dreamt of seven large heads of grain being swallowed by seven smaller and dryer ones. I need you to explain the meaning of these dreams to me."

But nobody could. Suddenly, the cupbearer exclaimed, "Joseph! He can help!"

Pharaoh summoned Joseph straight away.

At last, Joseph left his cell and met with the pharaoh face to face. But Joseph wasn't worried or scared. He knew that God was with him. Joseph listened to the king's dream and he replied. "My God will be able to give you its meaning."

He then explained, "The seven fat cows and large heads of grains represent seven years of plenty. There will be so much food in the whole of Egypt. Unfortunately, this will be followed by seven years of famine. I recommend that during the seven years of plenty, you save some of the food for the bad years to come."

Pharaoh was astonished by Joseph's wisdom, and he put him in charge of the food distribution. Joseph became a very important person.

And once again, things went just as Joseph had predicted. Seven years of bountiful crops were followed by seven years of no food. But Joseph, who knew that this was coming, had been saving plenty of food to get by during those years.

People from other countries traveled for days, hoping to be able to buy some of the food that Egypt had saved.

Amongst those people, there was a group of young men whom Joseph knew very well...

When Joseph saw his brothers, he was relieved to see that they didn't recognize him, and when they bowed down to him, he realized that his dreams from years ago had just come true.

"Are you spies?" queried Joseph. "No, we're not! We're here to buy food to feed our families back at home," they replied. And they told Joseph about their father, Jacob and their younger brother Benjamin, who stayed home. "If what you say is true, bring Benjamin to me," said Joseph, who missed his little brother and wanted to check that he was ok. The brothers whispered amongst themselves, "This is God punishing us for what we did to our brother Joseph," and they repented for what they did.

Joseph overheard and was very touched.

When the brothers told their father Jacob what happened, Jacob was terrified, "You're not going to take Benjamin with you! It's too dangerous!" he said. But in the end, with much hesitation, Jacob let him go.

When Joseph saw his brother, he was very happy, and he organized a big party for them all. But he wanted to test how changed his brothers really were, so he came out with a cunning plan. He hid a silver cup in Benjamin's sack of grain, and when it was time for the brothers to go, he said, "My cup! Somebody stole my cup! And whoever did it, will become my slave forever!"

When the brothers realized that the cup was inside Benjamin's sack, they couldn't believe their eyes. "Please, don't take Benjamin, take us instead!" they said.

Seeing his brothers protecting little Benjamin made Joseph understand that they had really changed. He was so moved that cried out, "I am your brother, Joseph!"

His brothers looked at him, surprised and terrified at the same time. Joseph comforted them, "Don't worry," he said, "I have forgiven you. God has used a bad situation to make something good. Now I can rescue my entire family from the famine."

And he did. As every member of his family, including his elderly father Jacob, was invited to move to Egypt.

When Jacob and Joseph met after all those years, they gave each other the biggest hug and they praised God together. They thanked Him for His provision and for the way that He had shown mercy and love.

Joseph introduced him to his wife and children and together, they started a new chapter of their lives, confident in God's provision for the years to come.

Paperback First Edition ISBN: 978-1-62931-035-0

Written by Rev. Roycos Hom.

Translated by Laura Caputo-Wickham.

Illustrated by Yuling Deng.

First printing edition 2018.

J Gospel Net Inc.
22 Howard Street, Bsmt C,
New York, NY 10013 USA

www.jgospel.com

J GOSPEL

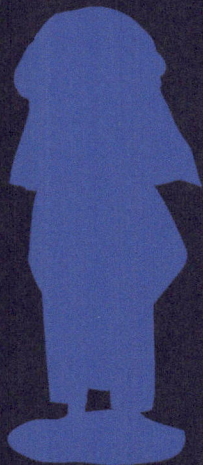

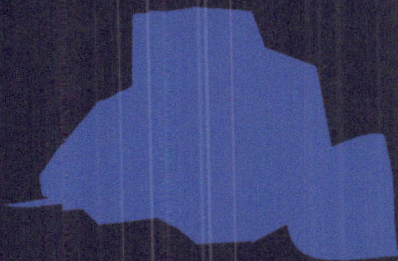

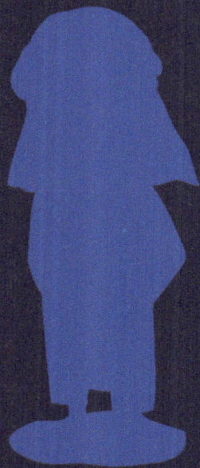

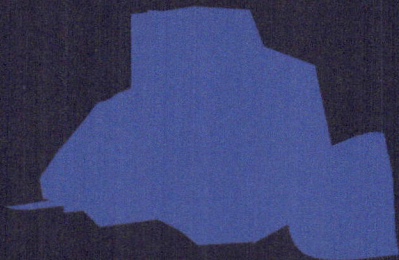

www.ingramcontent.com/pod-product-compliance
Lightning Source LLC
Chambersburg PA
CBHW040024050426
42452CB00003B/131